KINSHIP:
It's All Relative

KINSHIP

It's All Relative

by

Jackie Smith Arnold

Contents

Dedicated to Bill who encouraged me,
To my ancestors who created me,
To my descendants who will try to explain me,
To my collateral relatives who will be surprised.

Thank you to Helen Bobowski and Tom Kootsillas for their early support, and an extra special thank you to Janet Dyki, Elk Township Librarian, who always found the extra bit of information I needed.

1 • The Beginnings of Kinship

As it was in the beginning . . .

What is kinship?

Webster says kinship is *"the quality or state of being in a relationship, usually in a blood relationship."* But is there more to kinship than a definition?

Robert Frost said, "Home is the place, when you go there, they have to take you in." Home—whether it's a house or an emotional state—is where we find our relatives; our kin, blood of our blood.

Relatives are people we get stuck with at birth, for better or worse; chapels of pride or citadels of shame. They must be invited to family reunions, and notified of funerals. Relatives share ancestors and sit beside each other on the family tree. They are near and far, shirt-tail and kissin' kin, and all degrees in between.

Why is blood relationship of great interest to some, while others couldn't care less? Who is your "next of kin?" What about relatives more distant? Have you ever wondered why some cousins are removed and others are not?

Why are there prohibitions against marrying kin? And does the legal definition of incest change to suit social mores, or to pander to the whims of powerful personalities? For instance, the Roman emperor Claudius forced repeal of the senate's law against uncle/niece marriages to allow him to marry his niece,

1

Agrippina, thereby making it possible for her son, Nero, to fiddle while Rome burned.

Do children born of modern technology (through a surrogate mother, in vitro fertilization, or artificial insemination) have legal rights to know their biological background and socialize with their "kin?" Do genes carry the secrets to personality, health, and longevity? Why does the law require a husband to accept as his own any child born to his legal wife?

Let's open the door of kinship and see who's been taken in.

Why does kinship matter?

Kinship, degrees, removed! Are you confused, perplexed, or bored when it comes to determining how close your relatives are? And if it's all that confusing, forget it—who cares?

Believe it or not, some people are more interested in your **pedigree** (a register recording lines of ancestors) than in your astrological birth sign. The Daughters of the American Revolution *demand* a proper pedigree. Genealogical societies not only need kinship, they swear by it.

And there are compelling reasons to be interested in kinship. Personality traits may be inherited more often than previously thought. For example, a couple may be mild, quiet people and have raised several children who are all like themselves except for one. The exception is a child who is loud, aggressive, and temperamental. Mom and Dad search their hearts wondering where they went wrong, never realizing those traits are embedded in the child's genes, and the characteristics inherited from a distant ancestor.

When a young fiancée says, "I don't like his family, but it doesn't matter, I'm not marrying them," it's time to worry. You *do* marry your spouse's family. The person you choose to spend your life with is a composite of his or her family's social experience and **genetic** (kinship) history. Your spouse may not currently manifest undesirable traits, but with the wrong stimuli or pressures, could revert to inherited or learned ways of coping. By analyzing lovable characteristics along with any faults of the prospective in-laws, a couple can face potential problems and address questions about the future.

To isolate the individual from his kinship group and family in the name of love is to bury one's head in the sand. The apple doesn't fall far from the tree, they say, and the prickly pear tree produces only prickly pears.

How the family got started

By the act of being born we acquire a family, and the unifying ingredient of family life is kinship. Like most people, we probably don't think much about (or sometimes of) this group of Homo sapiens, or how they impact upon us. Oh, we may occasionally wonder how we got stuck with a particularly motley crew when John Doe down the street got all the winners, but that's about it.

Kinship ties probably began when our early ancestors entered the caves. **Paternal** (through the father) kinship was late in developing. A female had no way of knowing who fathered her child, and the male was unaware of his role in procreation, because sex was not understood as relevant to reproduction. With no estrous period (a specific time when an animal is in heat), the human female was available to the male at whim, and the long gestation removed the moment of conception a considerable distance from birth. Children were tremendously important to the small bands of struggling humanity, so birth was more significant than conception. Out of necessity, **matrilineal** (through the mother) kinship was the only form observed.

If an imaginary female named Ana had scratched her family tree on the cave wall, she would have provided an idea of how **cognate** (related on the mother's side) kinship was observed (figure 1).

As long as Ana's daughters produced females, Ana's line of descent remained recognizably intact. If the great-granddaughter produced only sons, the ability to trace Ana's line would cease. Remember the link between Ana and her offspring could only be traced through females descended from her.

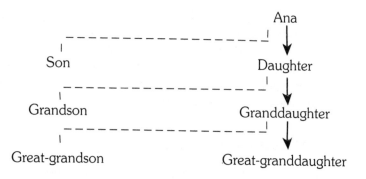

Figure 1 • Cognate kinship family tree

A new theory concludes that every person living today is descended from one African female who walked the earth 140,000 to 280,000 years ago.

A peculiarity in cell structure permits only women to pass one class of genes, carried by mitochondrial DNA, to offspring. University of California professor Allan C. Wilson says, "Each of us, men and women, got our mitochondrial DNA only from our mother, and she from her mother, and her mother from her mother, all the way back."

Consider the implications. We may not be sisters and brothers, but we are at least fiftieth cousins to every other person on earth today.

Enter the patriarchy

Man, never long content on the sidelines, became aware of his role in reproduction sometime during the neolithic era. This realization may have been the catalyst which made him recognize he possessed some amazing attributes: a voice capable of communication, an ability by virtue of his strength to control the females and children, and most important, the capability to create his "own" offspring.

Equality of roles may have been the norm when the male role in fertilization was unknown, but if so, existing social structure changed, probably once man realized his contribution in begetting children. Picture early man whooping and hollering and carrying on, laughing and dancing and singing: "Me, me, I did it," he shouts to the moon. See the female sitting near the fire, mouth agape, wondering what all the commotion is about, never suspecting that her way of life has been totally altered.

The male pauses, looks about, considers the act which he has so freely shared with the other males, and suddenly realizes the need to restrict particular females to himself. How else to know if the child from a woman's womb was the seed of his loins? Patriarchy and the male ego were born.

Concurrently, the patriarchal "family" unit began to co-operate with other embryonic groups. Small bands joined with other "families" to form **clans.** Clans coalesced into **tribes.**

Phratries are large kinship alliances within a tribe of clans. A smaller, more cohesive kindred group within a phratry is called a **sib** (or **sept**), which consists of all persons descended from a real or supposed ancestor. The Old English word "sibb," meaning kinship or kinsman, is the root word of sib and also of **sibling** (brother or sister).

The important role of kinship continuously developed and enlarged. Kinship determined to which family, sib, sept, clan, phratry, and tribe one belonged, and with whom one could mate. Where **endogamy** (breeding within the social group) had been practical, **exogamy** (breeding outside the basic social group) became possible and preferable.

Perhaps the first sexual taboo was invented when tribal leaders needed ways to prevent excessive inbreeding in the interest of survival; therefore mating with certain relatives (incest) was forbidden. How better to control male and female sex drive than to channel it outward in the direction best suited for the union of diverse, yet similar, groups?

Nutrition improved when humans settled down to farm, and the world experienced a population explosion. Human development took a giant leap forward when **outbreeding** (bringing new blood into the kinship line) became possible on a grand scale. As the population increased, so did the possible number of mates from which to choose. It became absolutely necessary to have a way of ensuring the incest taboo was not broken. "Rememberers" were trained to commit family information to memory and, at the time of any sexual pairing, were called forth to recite the ancestral line of the couple. If all went well and no impediment was found, the couple was united by whatever rites of passage were prescribed.

Monogamy and the male line

How was man to insure the paternity of a particular child, especially a son, and know the identity of all progeny born into his family unless he carefully guarded the women with whom he mated? Like a small child just beginning to understand the idea of "mine," man's possessiveness now demanded **monogamy** (having only one mate) from the females associated with him.

The patriarchal kinship system functions only if men exercise strict control over women's sexual activity, so man got busy and found ways to do just that. He veiled, girdled, spied upon, and cloistered his women.

Man's feeling of superiority became entrenched in secular and religious laws, and in marital customs. Where kinship had previously been traced by cognate descent (female lineage), **agnatic** descent (male lineage) became the accepted form.

Marriage

By marriage, a couple creates a family (a legal continuation of their respective kinship lines) and enters regulated society. All societies have a stake in the way a family conducts itself, and exercises some control over marriage.

Marriage distinguishes lawful unions, designates a father, and legitimizes the children. Recognition gives a child ancestors, a family name, a knowledge of kinship connections, and legal rights.

You may choose a mate, dress up in your best finery, invite relatives and friends, and reserve the chapel, but if you don't meet all requirements of various state and federal legislation, you aren't going to get married.

Western law considers marriage a binding contract whereby one man and one woman with the legal capacity to enter such an agreement promise to live together for life, or until the marriage is legally terminated.

- The **ceremonial marriage** is a wedding ceremony performed in accordance with the law of the state in which it takes place.

- **Common law marriage** is a private arrangement without a wedding ceremony or observance of legal requirements. If the couple conduct themselves as married in society at large, they are usually considered married in the eyes of the law. Some states refuse to sanction this form of cohabitation.

- The **consensual marriage** requires spoken vows confirming the couple's intent. After the words are spoken, the couple don't have to live together. The difference between common law marriage and consensual marriage is that vows are not required in a common law union.

- Special permission is necessary to contract a **proxy marriage** because it is allowed only in unusual circumstances which might keep the participants apart. Substitutes take the vows for the couple in absentia. Most states discourage this practice.

- **Miscegenation** is the name for marriage or cohabitation between people of different races or nationalities. Anti-miscegenation laws have been ruled unconstitutional by the United States Supreme Court.

- Pssst—want to hear a secret? There's a marriage ceremony that most people aren't aware of. It's called— guess what?—a **secret marriage**. The secret marriage is legal but quiet. To publicize a secret marriage is a misdemeanor.

You may ask who would want a secret marriage. Well, persons in police work often use this method of marriage to escape public attention that might lead a vindictive criminal to their doors. Couples who have held themselves as married to family and friends may slip away and secretly formalize their union.

The reasons for a secret ceremony are as varied as the couples who seek it. It's a binding and legal marriage, and must be dissolved legally as any other would be. Sorry, there is no secret divorce.

If you're contemplating a secret marriage, check with the proper authorities in your state. Sometimes a secret marriage is so hush-hush, it's difficult to find a magistrate who knows about it. If your reasons are compelling, keep trying.

There are as many forms of marriage as there are cultures to approve. In some parts of India and Sri Lanka, couples may contract a **benna marriage** whereby the husband enters the wife's kinship group and has little authority in the household.

In ancient Rome, **coemptio marriage** was a ceremony that symbolized the sale of a woman to a man and brought her under his power. Women frequently entered coemptio marriages to displace the jurisdiction of their guardians. The Roman ceremony of **confarreation** gave special sanctity to the marriage and conferred upon the husband absolute control over his wife as if she were his daughter. A confarreation marriage could only be dissolved by a ceremony of **diffareation** (an ancient form of divorce).

Ancient Hebrews practiced a compulsory system known as **levirate marriage** which required marriage of a widow to her late husband's brother, or in special circumstances to her husband's heir. This arrangement attempted to ensure the continuation of the deceased brother's bloodline by proxy.

When England's King Edward VIII decided to marry Wallis Warfield Simpson, a twice-divorced American, he proposed a **morganatic marriage** whereby Mrs. Simpson would become his legal wife but would not hold the rank of queen. Any children born of the union would not succeed to his titles, fiefs, or entailed property. The arrangement was rejected, and the King then abdicated his throne for "the woman I love."

There is a right to marry which cannot be casually denied, and states must have valid reasons to prohibit marriage. Most states require some form of prior intent such as a license. Both parties must be of legal age and sound mind. Every state in the union has some prohibition against marriage between close relatives, and all forbid marriage to a child or grandchild, parent or grandparent, uncle or aunt, niece or nephew, including illegitimate and half-blood relatives of the same degrees.

Various states extend the ban to first cousins, first cousins once removed, certain in-laws, certain step-relatives, grandaunt and granduncle, grandniece and grandnephew. Exceptions are sometimes made for religious reasons if the couple is no closer than first cousin.

Wisdom dictates the necessity to ascertain the laws of the state in which you plan to marry. By complying with the laws of society, observing the customs of religion (considered optional by those who do not value the role of religion), and confronting myriad responsibilities, you are ready to begin your own family and to legally continue your kinship line. You and your spouse will leave your **family of orientation** (the family of one's parents and relatives) and become a **family of procreation** (the family created by marriage). By marriage you acquire a new set of relatives who will be your **family of affinity**—the birth (kin group) family of one's spouse.

2 • Kinship Groups

*Oh, Lord: help me. If you don't, I'll ask my uncle
in New York.*

Jewish folk saying

Belonging to a family

Families are based on kinship; members belong by blood
(birth), by affinity (marriage), or through the courts (adoption).
In adoption, the adoptee becomes a legally accepted member
of the biological family with the same rights of inheritance as
a person born to the family. One exception may be the inheritance of an ancestral estate which, by prior will or entail, must
descend to a "blood" relative.

Some families extend a special affection to special friends
under the umbrella of **fictive kinship.** These people are
treated with deference and respect even to the point of using
familial terms when addressing them.

Sometimes a person lives with a family but isn't a member by
blood, marriage, or adoption. In this situation, the designation
is **foster-child** or **foster-parent.** (Technically, the term **parent**
is reserved for one's mother and father, but general usage has
enlarged the meaning to include grandmother and grand-
father, and others acting in the parental stead.)

Some primitive societies, in their innate wisdom, made use
of foster relationships by traditionally sending children to live
with maternal or paternal uncles and aunts. The idea seemed
to be that by removing the emotional anxiety felt by the natural
parents, the child more easily matured.

Types of family

In the United States, family life is defined by the **nuclear family.** Married couples with their children establish separate homes from and are financially independent of the couple's parents. However, kin ties are still extremely important.

If married children and their offspring live with the parents, the family is called an **extended family.** An extended family also includes aunts, uncles, and cousins along with grandparents, grandchildren, and others even if they live in separate homes. Many cultures assiduously maintain extended family ties.

Many countries, including Scotland and Ireland, recognize a large kinship group known as a **clan.** They maintain a strong interest in preserving clan history and traditions.

Tribal societies such as those of the Middle, Near, and Far East, plus some Latin countries, place greater emphasis on the extended family than do societies consisting mainly of nuclear families. It's usual in tribal societies to receive widows, divorced people, or never-married women into the bosom of the family, and to provide homes for elderly relatives.

When parents equally share the responsibility of a family, the unit is called an **equalitarian** or **egalitarian family.** Depending on which marital partner you speak to, such a family may or may not exist.

If a male heads the family, it's a **patriarchal family.** A **matriarchal family** is led by a female. A dictatorship is a family ruled by a two-year-old child. Just ask any couple that has one!

The **stepfamily** comes into existence when a divorced or widowed parent remarries. The new spouse becomes a stepparent to the children of the former marriage. Folklore has traditionally maligned the stepmother; consider the reputations of the stepmothers of Cinderella and Snow White. Conversely, stepchildren usually are portrayed as beautiful, lovable, and perfect. According to the stories, Cinderella and Snow White never left their clothes lying around the castle, refused to eat their dinner, or wrecked the family coach, or we might better understand the actions of the substitute parent.

Offspring from the couple's prior marriages become step-brothers and stepsisters. Children who share a single biological parent are **half-brothers** and **half-sisters**.

Ascents and descents

Kinship is figured **bilaterally** in the United States, which means an individual is affiliated with and descent traced through relatives on both the maternal and the paternal sides. Normally, the kinship circle is confined to a small group of kin consisting of grandparents, aunts, uncles, and cousins. The members of this group are considered one's kindred.

Kinship boundaries expand and contract depending on what some people call the "rich relative syndrome (RRS)." Under RRS, expansion in the kindred network allows inclusion of a shirt-tail third cousin once removed who is rich or famous, and contraction occurs when infamy rears its ugly head in the form of a first cousin.

In some societies, a descent group is traced **unilineally** through either the mother or the father. Rights and respon-sibilities are more clearly delineated than in Western societies using bilateral descent.

Obviously, the study of kinship pays particular attention to **ascents** and **descents**, from which we derive **ancestors** and **descendants**. Ascents (up from the self or ego) and descents (down from an ancestor) are of two types: **lineal** and **collateral**.

Lineal

Lineal descent is a direct or straight line from parent or grand-parent to child or grandchild. **Lineal ascent** is from the self or ego in a straight line to parent or grandparent (figure 2).

Lineal descents/ascents are **immediate** and **mediate**. An immediate lineal descent is from parent to child, and mediate lineal descent is from grandparent to grandchild. A descent is immediate only when there is no intervening link between ancestor and descendant.

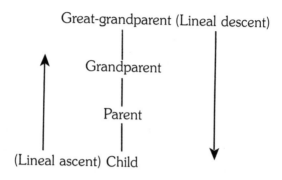

Great-grandparent (Lineal descent)

Grandparent

Parent

(Lineal ascent) Child

Figure 2 • Lineal descent and ascent

Collateral

In addition to grandparents, parents bequeath to their children another group of relatives known as **collaterals**; the kinship line is oblique rather than straight.

Collateral blood relatives are neither descendants nor ancestors in the *strictest* sense of the word. The term collateral kindred is used to designate brothers, sisters, uncles, aunts, nieces, nephews, and cousins. Collaterals descend from a common antecedent but can neither ascend to nor descend from other collateral relatives.

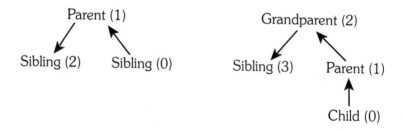

Parent (1)

Sibling (2)   Sibling (0)

Grandparent (2)

Sibling (3)   Parent (1)

Child (0)

Figure 3 • Collaterals over two generations

Figure 4 • Collaterals over three generations

Figure 3 shows the connection between collaterals. Starting with one sibling (0), the line ascends to the common ancestor and descends to the other sibling (2).

In figure 4 the line ascends from child (0), to parent (1), to grandparent (2), and down to parent's sibling (3). The numbers in parentheses represent the **degree of relationship**, which is explained more fully in the next chapter.

Three families at once

Kinship in the first instance is that which belongs to one by birth, and refers to origin or descent, birthright, or inheritance. Kinship is based on the biological blood we share with others. When someone says, "Blood is thicker than water!" they proclaim their first loyalties lie with family members.

Our place in the family structure is determined by the degree (amount) of blood we share with others. But we can simultaneously belong to three different kinship groups. Life begins in a **family of orientation** (parents, their offspring, and other parental relatives). When we marry, we establish a **family of procreation** (for purpose of having children), and through our spouse we gain a **family of affinity** (the kinship group to which our spouse belongs). These three families deserve a new chapter.

3 • Our Three Families

[Aunt Alexandra] *never let a chance escape her to point out the shortcomings of other tribal groups to the greater glory of our own, a habit that amused Jem rather than annoyed him: "Aunty better watch how she talks—scratch most folks in Maycomb and they're kin to us."*

Harper Lee, *To Kill a Mockingbird*

Family of orientation

By birth, we belong to a family of orientation; the family of our parents and their relatives. We are who we are because they are who they are. From them we inherit our physical and emotional characteristics such as disposition, eye color, body structure, and facial features. Blame those protruding teeth or that big nose on some long-forgotten ancestor if it makes you feel any better, but don't forget to thank them for a beautiful smile, flirtatious dimple, or gorgeous red hair.

The family of orientation is the only family that can't be chosen. We carry the inherited genes around like so much baggage, and wouldn't mind a bit if parts of it were lost en route. Even when we believe we have successfully performed self-surgery on certain characteristics, the child or grandchild arrives as a reminder that the tendencies are waiting in the wings.

Siblings-german (children born of the same parents—the word "german" means full or whole, and is becoming obsolete) are the closet blood relatives, with the possible exception of **identical twins** (children conceived simultaneously as a division

17

of the ovum.) **Fraternal twins** (children conceived from separate ova) are no closer genetically than children individually born. See figure 5.

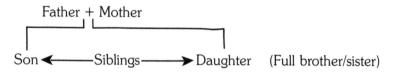

Son ◄———Siblings———► Daughter   (Full brother/sister)

Figure 5 • Full siblings or siblings-german

Within the family of orientation we first look to our parents, and to their parents. From self or ego, the direct line ascends to parents (the **parental** generation), grandparents (the **grand** generation), great-grandparents (the **great-grand** generation), adding a **great** for each preceding generation.

Patrilineal ascendancy is through the father, and matrilineal through the mother. Your father's relatives are paternal kin, your mother's relatives are maternal kin. You are a descendant of these relatives, and conversely they are your áncestors (figure 6).

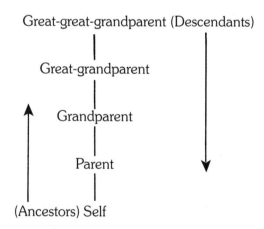

Figure 6 • Direct line of ascent/descent

Degrees of relationship

The chart of consanguinity (figure 7) shows the **degrees of relationship** between Self (0) and other relatives. Attorneys use charts similar to this one to determine next of kin and degree of relationship for purposes of distribution of property in intestate cases (where someone has died without leaving a will). They also use these charts to determine the degrees within which marriage is prohibited (incest), and as a basis for allowing certain relatives to testify against each other.

Notice that some relatives have the same degree of relationship to Self. For example: grandnephews/nieces (4), first cousins (4), granduncles/aunts (4) and great-great-grandparents (4). All of these relatives are in the fourth **degree of kinship** (or **consanguinity**) to Self.

The arrows linking Self to descendants and ancestors indicates lineal relatives. All others are collaterals.

Confused? Don't worry! In the rest of this section we'll work gradually through what all the relationships are called and what the names mean.

Aunts and uncles

The brother or sister of your parents is respectively your uncle (male) or your aunt (female). In some societies, paternal uncles and aunts have more status than maternal uncles and aunts.

At one time an unrelated woman addressed as aunt would have been insulted. The term implied that she was an old crone or a prostitute. Evolution has worked its magic and the term is now perfectly respectable.

On the other hand, an uncle was a man whose wisdom and help were sought. A children's game sometimes ended with the vanquished forced to cry "Uncle!" This in effect acknowledged the winner as wiser and definitely stronger than the loser. Crying uncle was the only way to get a bully off one's chest. Do children of today still do that?

"Uncle" was also a slang term for pawnbrokers. That makes sense if a person had no real uncle to turn to in time of trouble.

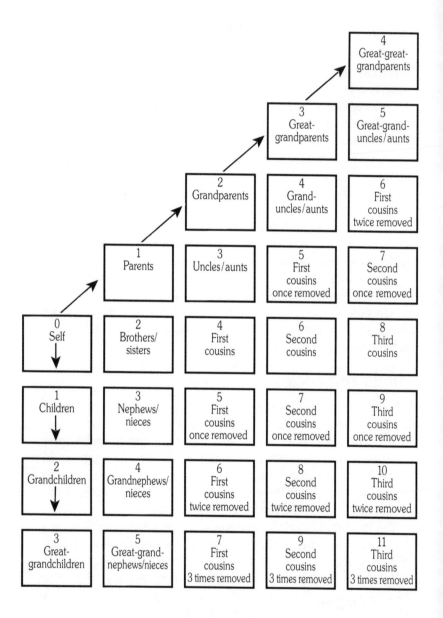

Figure 7 ● Chart of consanguinity

Then, of course, there is Uncle Sam, the cartoon symbol of the United States. He's a skinny, goateed fellow dressed in the national colors who tells the populace exactly what the government expects of them. To "speak like a Dutch uncle" has come to mean giving someone a disciplinary talking-to. The same message from an aunt is known as nagging.

Nieces and nephews

You will be recognized by your uncle and aunt as either **niece** (female) or **nephew** (male).

"Nephew" is an interesting word which archaically meant grandson or any male descendant. The word is taken from French *nepote* and Latin *nepos*. Similarly, "niece" came via French from Latin *neptis*, meaning granddaughter. *Nepote* and *nepos* also contributed the word "nepotism." Nepotism means favoritism shown to nephews and other relatives by reason of consanguinity rather than merit. Nepotism is practiced more often in the private sector than in the public sector. However, we usually see more merit in our relatives than do outsiders. There are some people whose good qualities can only be recognized by relatives, particularly when there is pressure from Aunt Nellie to give Nephew Ned Nerd a job. After all, if you won't favor your relatives, who will? And look at it this way, if God hadn't wanted us to prefer our relatives, he wouldn't have given us any.

Incidentally, in some African tribal societies there is no word for aunt, uncle, or cousin. The children of your siblings are considered to be your children as though you had conceived them. You're expected to accept responsibility whenever there's a need. The children of siblings describe each other as brother and sister instead of "cousin." The children address as mother and father not only their biological parents, but the parental siblings.

Generations

Parents and their siblings belong to one generation and their respective offspring to another. In kinship, **one generation is**

a single step in the line of descent from an ancestor. A mother can give birth to two children twenty years apart, but the siblings will always be in the same kinship generation. This is unlike social generations, which are made up of persons of similar ages.

The example of siblings whose births are separated by many years demonstrates how a person belongs to several different generations simultaneously. By birth, children are bound together in their kinship generation, but each will grow up in vastly different social and work generations.

Regardless of the time span between siblings, neither the family titles nor the kinship generations change. A woman who finds herself giving birth about the same time as does her daughter or daughter-in-law bears a child who enters the world as an aunt or uncle to her new grandchild.

Greats and grands

The siblings of your grandparents will be your **grandaunts** and **granduncles**. It's a mistake to lump them in with the "greats." What does the term "great aunt" mean? Does it mean a sister of a grandparent or a sister of a great-grandparent? Mixing the generations causes confusion. Some reference books designate a grandaunt as a great aunt, which compounds the problem since we expect more accuracy from the experts.

With the grands and the greats, this is the sequence: **grand**parent, **great-grand**parent, **great-great-grand**parent. Continue adding a great for every preceding generation. The same follows for grandaunt and granduncle, and grandniece and grandnephew. After the grands come the great-grands.

- *Great-grand*uncles/aunts are siblings of *great-grand*parents
- *Grand*uncles/aunts are siblings of *grand*parents
- *Uncles*/aunts are siblings of parents
- *Self*

Each line above represents one generation.

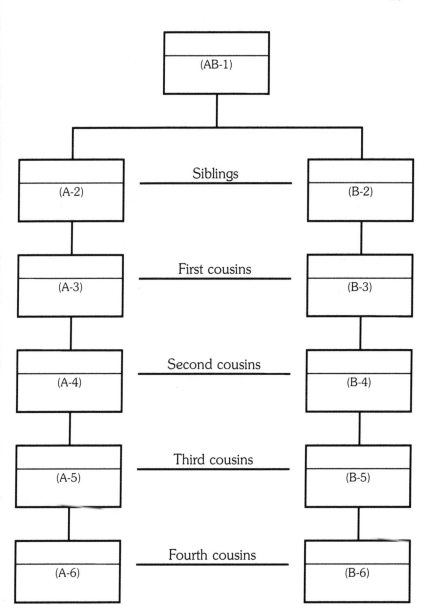

Figure 8 ● Relationship diagram

Cousins

Cousins share a common grandparent, with the degree of cousinship dependent on how the grandparent is shared (figure 8).

- Siblings *share* a parent.
- First cousins *share* a grandparent.
- Second cousins *share* a great-grandparent.
- Third cousins *share* a great-great-grandparent.
- Fourth cousins *share* a great-great-great-grandparent.
- Fifth cousins *share* a great-great-great-great-grandparent (and so on).

Another way to determine cousins is to look at aunts and uncles. The children of your aunts and uncles are your **cousins-german** or **first cousins**. In figure 9, grandparent (2) is a common ancestor of the self, parent, aunt/uncle, and child.

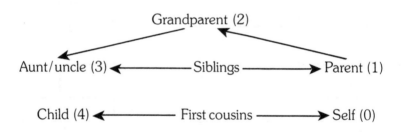

Figure 9 • First cousins, or cousins-german

Quarter cousins are properly in the **fourth degree** of consanguinity (that is, first cousins), but the term has come to express any remote degree of relationship, and even to bear an ironical significance in which it denotes a very trifling degree of kinship. Quarter is a term often corrupted to **cater**, which refers to the four spots on dice or cards.

The removes

If your first cousin has a child, the child becomes your **first cousin once removed**. The removes seem to create considerable difficulty. A question frequently asked is, "Removed from whom and to where?" No, it doesn't refer to the situation where someone demands, "Remove that child at once."

Simply put, removed means that a person belongs to a different kinship generation. A first cousin once removed is one generation removed from the source—a first cousin. Think of it as linguistic shorthand: "My first cousin once removed," instead of "My first cousin's child is one kinship generation removed from our original first cousin relationship."

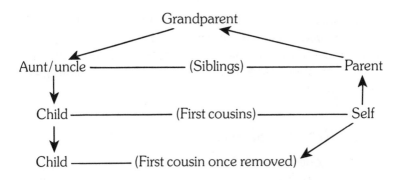

Figure 10 • **First cousins once removed**

For example, in figure 10 the sibling of Self's parent is Self's aunt or uncle. The child of the aunt or uncle is Self's first cousin. The child of Self's first cousin is a first cousin once removed to Self. Self's grandparent is the great-grandparent of Self's first cousin once removed. They are cousins by virtue of a shared grandparent by different degrees.

The child of Self's first cousin once removed is a first cousin twice removed (see figure 11). Each new generation will continue to be another step removed from the original first cousin relationship.

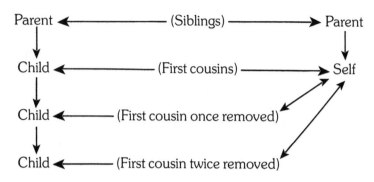

Figure 11 • First cousins twice removed

Ask yourself, "Who is John to me?" If you know that John's mother is your third cousin, then John is your third cousin once removed. If John is your third cousin once removed, one of your great-great-grandparents will be John's great-great-great-grandparent.

Calculating cousinhood

How does one acquire second cousins? By being the respective children of first cousins. In figure 11, Self had no children. Let's see what will happen if Self has a child (figure 12).

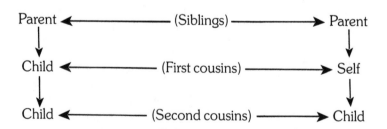

Figure 12 • Second cousins

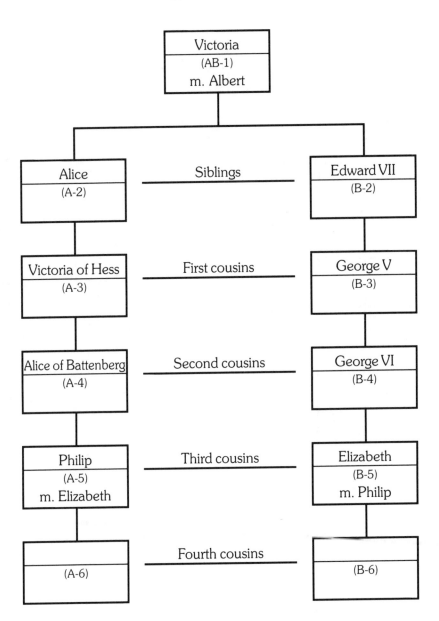

**Figure 13 ● Relationship diagram for
Queen Elizabeth II and Prince Philip**

Relationship Table A

to B

Relationship of A	AB-1	B-2	B-3	B-4	B-5	B-6
AB-1		Parents	Grandparent	Great-grandparent	Great-great-grandparent	Great-great-great-grandparent
A-2	Child	Brother/sister	Aunt/uncle	Grand-aunt/uncle	Great-grand-aunt/uncle	Great-great-grand-aunt/uncle
A-3	Grandchild	Niece/nephew	First cousin	First cousin once removed	First cousin twice removed	First cousin three times removed
A-4	Great-grandchild	Grand-niece/nephew	First cousin once removed	Second cousin	Second cousin once removed	Second cousin twice removed
A-5	Great-great-grandchild	Great-grand-niece/nephew	First cousin twice removed	Second cousin once removed	Third cousin	Third cousin once removed
A-6	Great-great-great-grandchild	Great-great-grandniece/nephew	First cousin three times removed	Second cousin twice removed	Third cousin once removed	Fourth cousin

1. To find the relationship of A to B, find the "A" code (e.g. A-4) of the individual, from the relationship diagram (figure 8).
2. Select the code in the left-hand column of the table above.
3. Read across the row to the desired column (e.g. B-5) to find the relationship.

Relationship Table B

to A

Relationship of B	AB-1	A-2	A-3	A-4	A-5	A-6
B-1		Parents	Grandparent	Great-grandparent	Great-great-grandparent	Great-great-grandparent
B-2	Child	Brother/sister	Aunt/uncle	Grand-aunt/uncle	Great-grand-aunt/uncle	Great-great-grand-aunt/uncle
B-3	Grandchild	Niece/nephew	First cousin	First cousin	First cousin twice removed	First cousin three times removed
B-4	Great-grandchild	Grand-niece/nephew	First cousin once removed	Second cousin	Second cousin once removed	Second cousin twice removed
B-5	Great-great-grandchild	Great-grand-niece/nephew	First cousin twice removed	Second cousin once removed	Third cousin	Third cousin once removed
B-6	Great-great-great-grandchild	Great-great-grandniece/nephew	First cousin three times removed	Second cousin twice removed	Third cousin once removed	Fourth cousin

4. To find the relationship of B to A, find the "B" code (e.g. B-4) of the individual, from the relationship diagram (figure 8).
5. Select the code in the left-hand column of the table above.
6. Read across the column to the desired row (e.g. A-5) to find the relationship.

Figure 14 • Relationship tables

Earlier we looked at another way to determine degrees of cousinhood through the grandparents. Let's review. Remember, **cousins are relatives who share a common grandparent.** Children of first cousins are second cousins, and offspring of second cousins are third cousins. To take an example (figure 13), Queen Elizabeth II of England married her third cousin, Philip Mountbatten (Battenberg). Elizabeth and Philip are related through the lineage of Queen Victoria, their common great-great-grandmother. This relationship places them in the eighth degree of consanguinity. The degree is calculated by starting with Elizabeth (0) and proceeding through the line of ascent to the nearest common progenitor, Victoria (4), and then down to the relative in question, Philip (8).

At various times in the past, this relationship might have been within the forbidden (incest) degrees for marriage purposes. It also means that Philip and Elizabeth are **third cousins once removed** to their own children.

Queen Victoria had nine children, and she judiciously arranged marriages for them with most of the royal families of Europe, so that an in-depth examination of her descendants reveals a jumble of kinship lines. You can use figure 14 to help you work out your own kinship lines.

Doubles, parallels and crosses

A unique relationship comes into existence when siblings of one family marry siblings of another family. For example, if the brothers Smith marry the sisters Jones, their offspring will be **double first cousins.** Genetically, their children will inherit from the same gene pool as if they were siblings. While regular first cousins share only one set of common ancestors, double first cousins share all lineal and collateral relatives. In addition to being double first cousins, the Smith/Jones children are also **parallel** (or **ortho**) **first cousins.**

Parallel cousins are the children of two brothers or two sisters. **Cross cousins** are the children of a brother and a sister. For example, my sister and I have children, therefore our children are cognate parallel cousins. My brother and I have children and our respective children are cross cousins (figure 15).

Arab Bedouin societies frequently place great importance upon the first male child of one brother having marital rights to female offspring of another brother. Cross cousin marriages do occur in Arabic societies but without the familial significance of agnatic parallel cousin marriages.

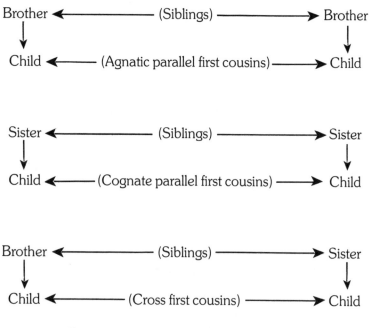

Figure 15 ● Parallel and cross cousins

Cousins who aren't cousins

"Cousin" seems to be used when it's a bother to delve into more complicated family relationships. When the English Crown issues writs or other formal instruments, the word "cousin" signifies any peer of the degree of earl.

The practice of addressing an earl as "cousin" began when Henry IV, related to or allied with every earl then in the kingdom, wearied of trying to keep each earl in the proper degree of kinship. Henry was concerned about hurt feelings and their possible consequences if he miscalculated a single degree, whole or removed, so he solved the problem by addressing all of them as "Dear cousin." The tradition holds while the reason has become lost in antiquity.

Maybe some African families have the right idea. Be done with the whole jumble of aunts and uncles and cousins by degree. Just call some people mom and dad, and all the others brother and sister.

In conclusion

Grandparents and the greats, father, mother, aunts, uncles, and cousins by degree—these are the members of our family of orientation. There is no choice involved. We can't divorce them, although we can disinherit them. We can love them, leave them, hate them, need them, avoid them, ignore them, and pretend they don't exist . . . and nothing changes; blood remains the same.

We must take them as we get them, and they often hang about our necks like albatrosses, getting in our way and embarrassing us at every opportunity. But what would we do without them? We look in their faces and see ourselves and our children. They share our rites of passage: weddings, births, deaths, happy times, sad times, laughter, and tears. They sing our lullabies and recite our goodnight prayers. They are there for us, and we for them. To paraphrase Pogo from his home in the swamp, "We have met our kindred and they are us."

Family of procreation

When we marry, we enter a family of procreation. This family is created by choice. Many people have lived to regret in leisure a spouse chosen in haste. Whether or not a couple actually produce offspring doesn't alter the terminology of the kinship purpose. It's within this family, if all goes well, we create our own descendants and become somebody's ancestor. Kinship; that's what makes the world go round.

In our family of procreation we are promoted from child of our parents to parent of our children. Our parents become grandparents, considered by some to be a fringe benefit of being a parent in the first place.

Family of affinity

Obviously, the object of your affection didn't spring forth like Venus rising from the sea foam. The only foam you will see is the sputtering of your intended's parents if they don't think you're good enough for their darling. Along with your mate comes a ready-made bevy of relatives, and like it or not, you've acquired another family.

The family of your spouse is your family of affinity, and the members are your **in-laws.** Your beloved's parents are your **mother-in-law** and **father-in-law.** Spousal siblings are your **brothers-in-law** and **sisters-in-law.** Technically, the husband or wife of a brother-in-law or sister-in-law is not an in-law; however, as a courtesy they are introduced as such.

All blood relatives of your spouse become your **affinity relatives,** and by adding the term "in-law" or the phrase "**by marriage**," we instantly identify to the world their place in our kinship circle. Usually, the term in-law is eliminated when addressing aunts, uncles, grandparents, and cousins. Most people introduce affinity relatives as Aunt Jane or Uncle Toby, unless Aunt Jane has fallen into the punch bowl, or Uncle Toby has gone skinny-dipping in the fishpond. Then it's perfectly acceptable to announce quite distinctly, "My *husband's* Aunt Jane and Uncle Toby really do know how to have a good time."

A family of affinity is ours only so long as we remain married to our spouse. Unfortunately, due to death or divorce, affinity relationships are often severed. Only the rare family can look beyond the problems of a couple, remain neutral, and stay on good terms with both parties.

If you're ever in the unhappy situation of divorce, spare your children the pain of separation from the family of your ex-spouse. Remember, they may have been your family of affinity, but they are your children's family of orientation.

From our family of orientation we learn who we are and where we came from. In our family of procreation we pass along the genes and learned behavior of past generations and continue kinship connections; and from our family of affinity we learn patience, forbearance, and tolerance, hopefully. God bless 'em all.

4 • Kinship and Your Health

Know thyself.

Inscription over the entrance of the
Temple of Apollo at Delphi

Inheritance is generally thought of as money or property which parents, relatives, or friends have distributed in the past, or possibly will leave in the future. Laws of inheritance are concerned with an orderly transfer of wealth between persons and from one generation to the next, but there is another bequest over which the courts, as yet, have no control. This comes as a gift we can't reject any more than an offer from the "Godfather" could be refused. Kinship plays a major role. Part of every ancestor is being repeated in some measure in each tiny fetus.

Your genetic inheritance

In many ways, receiving good **genes** is more important than inheriting stocks and bonds. All of us know people, or whole families, who seem to defy the laws of common sense when it comes to abusing their bodies, and they get away with it. Other individuals exercise, follow nutritious diets, maintain proper weight levels, neither smoke nor drink, and still contract some life-threatening ailment. Why?

The Oracle of the Chicken Gizzard was approached by a young man seeking the secret of a long and healthy life. The Oracle consulted the stars and tossed bones on the ground. She tested wind direction and gazed into a crystal ball. She brewed countless cups of strong coffee and swirled the grounds. She ate seven deep-fried chicken gizzards and meditated. She counted the letters in his name and reduced them to a single digit. She read his palm, searching the faint, squiggly lines for clues. She consulted tarot cards and rune stones. When she was at last exhausted by her efforts, she leaned forward; the young man held his breath.

She spoke.

"Choose your ancestors well."

Researching genetic disease

Until very recently "choose the correct ancestors" was the best advice medical science could give. Researchers are now looking for large, extended families in which certain illnesses are prevalent. By studying the healthy members and comparing them to members who have already developed a particular disease, scientists hope to predict medical trends.

- University of Utah scientists studied colon cancer by utilizing ancestral records of the Church of Jesus Christ of Latter-day Saints (Mormon Church). Comparing these genealogical histories with a statewide tumor registry, they discovered a family with almost 10,000 members whose colon cancer rate was unusually high. Through extensive testing along kinship lines, scientists found a gene which causes a predisposition to this cancer.

- Manic depression strikes regularly in certain Amish clans. Janice Egeland, a medical sociologist, hopes to isolate and compare the suspect gene with other family groups that either maintain extensive family records or have members with good memories. Researchers will then try to predict which members might become afflicted.

- People with West African heritage are particularly concerned with sickle cell anemia. This is a form of inherited chronic anemia, found mainly amongst those with West African ancestry, in which many of the red blood cells become sickle-shaped.

In the very near future, a fertilized egg only a few hours old may be tested for undesirable genes. If a problem is discovered, the ovum may be destroyed, depending upon the wishes of the parents.

Countless couples are already trying to ensure the conception of the physically and mentally perfect child, including choosing the child's sex. Recently, two Japanese professors developed a technique which guarantees the birth of females in families who have histories of male-related type diseases. In ordinary circumstances, male babies are socially preferred over female babies.

Results and problems

If genetic testing had been possible in 1864, would that glorious artist, Toulouse-Lautrec, have been aborted?

Henri Marie Raymond de Toulouse-Lautrec was born into a proud, ruling-class family with an unbroken line descending from father to son since the year 1196. Toulouse-Lautrec's parents were first cousins, and their only surviving son suffered from dwarfism. The couple blamed their familial relationship for their son's condition and they may have been right.

Modern medical studies conclude that Toulouse-Lautrec suffered a rare form of dwarfism (pyknodysostosis) which is more common in offspring of consanguineous (closely related) parents. Henri suffered abnormally short limbs; his features coarsened, his lips thickened, he drooled uncontrollably, and his nose dripped constantly. He became bitter, cynical, and alcoholic. Genetic testing prior to his birth could have alerted his parents, making one wonder what their choice might have been.

In the search for the perfect child, what will happen to the damaged zygotes, those unfortunate, fertilized eggs found to be defective? Will they be given a decent burial with grieving relatives at the grave site, or will they be thrown out with yesterday's garbage? Will their existence be recorded in a family history, or will they be used for experimentation? Who will speak for unborn Toulouse-Lautrecs, dwarfed, ugly, talented little creatures, or the idiot savants whose mental functions are severely limited except for that one special, exceptional talent? Through no fault of their own, they are victims of a tangled kinship web.

Genes and your personality

Behavioral patterns are also being carefully scrutinized. "Nature versus nurture" has been debated for centuries, but only now are controlled scientific experiments directing attention toward inherited tendencies of aggression and passivity. Perhaps a combination of nature *and* nuture is needed to cause problems to surface.

Close examination of adoptees is yielding information that points to the gene theory of inherited predisposition to behavior traits. One theory suggests that if a predisposition for criminal activity exists in the genes, then certain stimuli might exacerbate the tendency into a full-fledged problem.

Researchers at the Minnesota Center for Twin and Adoption Research say some personality traits are at least partly determined by heredity in addition to environment. Psychologists compared personality test results for identical twins to those for the general population and calculated the average contribution of genes to the following traits:

Trait	Contribution of genes (percent)
Extroversion	61
Conformity	60
Creativity	55
Paranoia	55
Worry	55
Optimism	54
Aggressiveness	48
Ambitiousness	46
Orderliness	43
Intimacy	33

- By an amazing coincidence, Billy the Kid, Wild Bill Hickok, the Dalton Brothers, the Younger Brothers, and Frank and Jesse James were all blue-eyed blonds. Scientists would certainly collect a wealth of information if they could examine those men to ascertain if the same gene that made the blue eyes and blond hair contributed to their aggressive and adventurous natures.
- The Tarahumare Indians of the Sierra Madres in Mexico never commit crimes. Scientists might feel they have inherited a gene with a predisposition for passivity, whereas sociologists probably think it's because the Tarahumare don't spank their children.

A cynical grandmother was asked the difference between heredity, environment, and kinship. She quipped, "If the baby looks like his father, that's heredity. If he looks like a neighbor, that's environment. If he's accepted by the family, that's kinship."

AI, in vitro, and surrogacy

Until recently, an infertile woman who desired a child had two choices: adjust to her barren state, or adopt. If she chose adoption, she had to accept the fact that the child would be the genetic product of two other people. The child would not be an actual link in her kinship chain.

Presently, a woman with an infertile husband can be **artificially inseminated** with another man's sperm—AI. Since the law considers the child of a married woman to be her husband's responsibility, there is no basic legal conflict.

What happens if both husband and wife are infertile? An embryo is created in a test tube using donated ovum and sperm (**in vitro fertilization**). The resulting fertilized egg is implanted in the wife's womb, and if all goes well, she will bear a child.

But wait! What happens if she couldn't carry a child to term, or if her uterus had been surgically removed? The woman could have her ovum collected, fertilized with her husband's sperm (or that of a donor), and placed in the womb of another woman—a **surrogate mother**. When the gestation period is complete, a healthy baby is born and turned over to the couple contracting for the service. Every one ignores the worn, tangled skein of kinship and lives happily ever after.

Or do they?

Ethical problems

How many people are involved in creating this child? The husband and wife, the sperm donor, the ovum donor, and the woman from rent-a-womb—references supplied. We won't even count the scientists, doctors, technicians, and lawyers who were necessary. Perhaps they can best be compared to the matchmakers of olden days.

Who are the real parents of this baby?

What would happen if just one person in this group reconsidered? Do the parents of the sperm donor have any rights to know and love their grandchild? Must they ignore the pull of their blood? Will the donor of the egg mourn the loss of her child? Will the biological mother who has carried the child for nine months feel guilt and grief when the child is placed in another woman's arms?

If a child conceived through surrogate parenting, in vitro fertilization, or artificial insemination ever wishes to have a meeting with its sperm father, its ovum mother, or its family of orientation, will the courts order this information revealed in all circumstances, or only when there is proof of medical necessity, or not at all?

What happens if the child is defective? Must the contracting party accept damaged goods? Should there be a "lemon law" for new born babies?

Noel Keane, a pioneer in surrogate law, requested a legal opinion to determine, in advance of a child's birth, the legal right of a couple to receive the child without resorting to adoption. In a landmark ruling, the judge ruled, subject to genetic testing, that the biological parents were the couple who had contributed the sperm and egg. This was the nation's first legal opinion in determining the parentage of a child conceived using in vitro fertilization in the womb of a surrogate mother. The interim order didn't become final until after the birth of a baby girl. During the interval, the child was legally parentless and without kindred.

Questions of ethics must be quickly resolved. We may eventually have a situation in which the contracting couple perishes together in an accident. The courts must decide if the child born posthumously to a surrogate mother is their legal heir. Who is responsible if it is determined that the child is not the genetic product of the couple? Can a surrogate be forced to raise a child when the contractors die before the contract is fulfilled? As Hardy, of Laurel and Hardy, would say, "It's a fine mess you've gotten us into!"

Medical charts

Until science perfects its techniques, we'll continue to play "gene roulette" unless we help ourselves by noting trends toward particular illnesses within our families. We can't wait for a research team to show up on our doorstep.

It's extremely important for families to compile a medical history. How often have you or a member of your family gone to the doctor and faced questions regarding personal or family health? Could you answer the queries?

If your family doesn't have a detailed medical history, why not appoint yourself medical historian? Become a kinologist!

The best way to begin is to compile a medical family tree. You will be concerned with blood relatives only. Talk with or write to relatives asking them to supply medical information about themselves and members of their families. There are charts you can use as examples at the end of this book.

Charts should also include any tendency toward substance abuse. Medical experts believe the proclivity for alcohol and drug abuse may be inherited.

Don't forget to include information about the family's mental health. Was a great-grandmother emotionally unstable? Is there a family history of Alzheimer's disease? If any family member committed suicide, make a note of it. In the event another relative begins to act in an unusual way, the knowledge might help you take action.

How did family members interact? Was the family situation fairly serene, or broken with conflict? Were any family members compulsively neat and clean, or the opposite, always slovenly and lazy, making everyone around them uncomfortable? Were most of the relatives middle of the road and moderate in their total behavior?

Was Aunt Zelda's drinking called the "vapors," and did the family ignore it, indicating a reluctance to face and deal with an unpleasant situation? Was an erratic and irrational relative allowed to disrupt the serenity of the family time after time without restraint? Continual refusal to deal with reality is an indication of the collective mental health of a family.

Don't worry about hurt feelings. After all, you don't plan to publish this information for the world to see. Your only purpose is to provide useful information to future generations.

Your family is made up of the good, the bad, the ugly, and the beautiful, so don't overlook the "good stuff." Allow space in your charts for talents.

If you record accomplishments without critical analysis, later generations will be warmed by the knowledge that a special talent, vocation, or avocation is shared with an ancestor. Learning that a long-departed relative had a particular talent may spur a great-grandchild to develop a latent talent of his own. Who knows what future genius is waiting for such inspiration?

By combining careful mate selection with genetic counseling (when indicated), and armed with a knowledge of family medical history, no one need play "gene roulette" with the lives of future kindred.

5 • Kinship and Children

Suffer the little children . . .

Matthew 19:14

How and where do orphans, foster children, foundlings, and bastards fit into kinship groups and family structure? How do they claim their places among their biological kindred?

Orphans, foster children, and foundlings

A person who has lost parents, or sometimes a child who has lost one (especially a father), is considered an **orphan.** When children are orphaned, there is no legal obligation on the part of their kindred to accept and nurture them, but ideally families make every effort to love and care for them.

To **foster** means to nurse or nurture, feed, or provide (hopefully) the love and protection that, for a variety of reasons, isn't forthcoming from natural parents. Fostering by choice is an ancient practice, and shouldn't be confused with court-sanctioned custodial care for which the caretakers are compensated by society.

In Ireland, and in several other societies, families occasionally sent their children to a "fosterer." The foster relationship was considered stronger than the original blood kinship.

Wet-nurses (women who breastfeed the children of other women) have always played an important part in family life. There is a belief in Middle Eastern countries that many traits and talents are instilled with mother's milk. Consequently, families vied for the services of the best nurses.

When the Prophet Mohammed was born, infants from influential homes were sent into the desert to be suckled and raised to adolescence. At the selection site, desirable wet-nurses refused to accept Mohammed because his family, while comfortable, was not extremely wealthy. Traditionally, the nurse's family benefited greatly if the suckling's kin had great wealth and power.

Finally, an undistinguished nurse took pity and accepted Mohammed into her family. She immediately began to experience a multitude of heavenly blessings which were considered omens of the child's future greatness. Needless to say, the other nurses regretted their own lack of foresight.

A **foundling** is a child deserted by its parents as a baby or an infant. In ancient societies, and maybe even a few modern ones, unwanted infants—especially girls—were abandoned and exposed to the elements much as some people drop off unwanted cats and dogs.

Broken kinship

Societies have always been troubled by the dilemma of homeless children cast adrift from kinship anchors. Unprotected minors were often treated with indifference or misguided solicitude. Even today, metropolitan areas are haunted by children who live by their wits.

Experiments were undertaken in New York in 1854 to locate rural homes for indigent and homeless minors. Almost 150,000 children were shipped on "orphan trains" to towns all over the Midwest before the programs ended in 1929.

Family ties were broken; kinship was severed, never to be mended in most cases. Numerous children who participated in the exodus were made ashamed by the attitude of the townspeople, and when they grew older preferred not to share their memories.

A lasting sense of rootlessness is created when children are deprived of their kinship circle, regardless of altruistic reasons.

Bastards

"He was as uncomfortable as a **bastard** at a family reunion."
Now that's mighty uncomfortable.

While bastards may have biological blood which connects
them to a particular family, the courts believe that nothing
must be allowed to interfere with cohesive, legal family structure.
Illegitimate children definitely interfere with family structure
and inheritance procedures. In order for a child born outside
of wedlock to take its place in a paternal kinship group, an
unmarried woman must present positive proof of her child's
paternity; unless she produces results of blood testing or genetic
analysis, or the man in question admits paternity, there isn't
much she can do to legally establish a particular man as the
father.

The law looks differently upon married women. Once a
couple marries, any child born during the marriage is considered
to be the husband's, and the child takes its rightful place within
the family. As a sage once said, no doubt speaking from experience, "It's a wise father who knows his own son" —or words
to that effect.

Perhaps we can now better understand why some societies
guard their females so zealously. By marriage, the male effec-
tively says he'll accept as his own any child born to his wife.
This acceptance gives a child the status of an heir, a paternal
name and paternal ancestors, rights under the law, and dignity
in a society that prizes formalities.

If a man denies paternity of a child born to his wife, he must
seek court action to remove the child from his responsibility.
The courts won't lightly deprive a child of its birthright, and
unimpeachable proof must be presented. In the past, confession
of the woman was about the only way to prove the child
wasn't her husband's, but today there are several methods,
such as genetic testing and blood analysis.

Man hasn't always resorted to the courts to dispose of a
child suspected to be the fruit of another man's loins. He
bashed the woman over the head a few times, tossed the babe

on a trash heap, and went back to family business as usual. If he'd been waiting for an excuse to dump her, he denounced her transgressions, and turned her over to the locals for stoning or some equally hideous demise.

Bastards in many earlier societies fared better than they currently do. Historians of fifteenth-century France and Germany consider that period to be the age of the bastard. Both male and female bastards were provided with the best the father could manage, and children born out of wedlock were generally well treated. A respected nobleman was shamed among his acquaintances if he ill-treated his extramarital offspring. Most nobles and gentlemen provided illegitimate sons with excellent educations and funds, and arranged good marriages for illegitimate daughters.

Bastards didn't do as well in Great Britain. In Europe, a bastard could be legitimized (see below) if his or her parents later married, but the English resisted the idea well into the 1960s. It's ironic that Henry VIII sired healthy, strong, male children outside the marital bed, but within it produced only girls and sickly sons who died either at birth or in early adolescence. To a man of Henry's ego, this was a blow of the greatest magnitude, for all the adoptions in the world would not have met the need to be of Henry's blood to succeed to the throne.

The basic difference between bastards and their legitimate siblings is the illegitimate ones can't inherit a family title, or any portion of the family estate that isn't freely given during the lifetime of the father.

To **legitimize** means to put a bastard in the position, or state, of a legitimate child before the law, by legal means; distinguished from adoption, which has no bearing to blood relationship. Acceptance of the child doesn't have to be spoken, but can be silent. Silence, when one is under a duty to speak, may be more effective than words. For example, if a child is accepted into a paternal family, this is considered evidence of public acknowledgement even though the father may remain silent.

Claims of kinship

A newspaper wag, with tongue in cheek and pen in hand, founded the Illegitimate Children of Public Officials Society of America. The most recent nominee is Steven Mark Brown, a Dallas man claiming to be the illegitimate son of the late President Lyndon B. Johnson. Brown is suing Lady Bird, Johnson's widow, for a share of the estate. Perhaps those persons claiming entertainment celebrities as parents should form a society of the Illegitimate Sons and Daughters of Movie Stars. Two women who claim to be the bastard daughters of Elvis Presley could be charter members.

Courts are sometimes confronted with the problem of people who believe they belong to certain families and wish to have familial acceptance—that is, to be accepted into the kinship circle, or at least share in the family estate.

Michigan's Frances Mealbach has filed a legal claim to a share of auto-magnate John Dodge's estate. She contends she's a separated Siamese twin of another Dodge daughter. She claims she and her twin sister were separated in a secret operation, and Frances was given to an adoptive family.

In the 1900s, Siamese twins were considered freaks, and Frances Mealbach believes this is why she was cast aside. She claims, among other things, that her adoptive family's fortunes improved dramatically after her adoption, that she has memories of being taken to a mysterious mansion where she visited only one or two people, that she bears scars which physicians say could have been produced by twin-separation surgery, and that her petitions to have the adoption records opened for study have been opposed by Dodge family attorneys.

Dodge attorneys declare the family member in question had no scars similar to Ms. Mealbach's, and they are treating the claim as a nuisance and/or a hoax. Because all the principal actors in this drama of family life except Ms. Mealbach are dead, the claimant must find something of substance in her adoption records to support her contentions. Until the release of adoption information, this matron has only her suspicions, her physical scars, and a perceived family resemblance to present as evidence at the jury trial she's requesting.

Caring for the children

Children, whether legitimate, illegitimate, foster, or foundling, deserve their places within family structures, preferably with their own kin group. Why should any child be deprived of a birthright because of the manner of birth?

The secrecy which surrounded adoptions is being eased as more children seek to know their birth families. Foster and adoptive parents are beginning to include the child's natural family in the child's upbringing. Many siblings, separated by adoption and divorce, are now being allowed to keep in touch.

Of course, children should be protected from violent or abusive parents under all circumstances, but they should be told the truth in a gentle and caring way. Adults should be careful not to make disparaging comparisons between a child and an absent parent.

Children are our links with the past, carriers of our genes, and the bridge to future generations. When the best laid plans go awry, let's love the children as they deserve and open our hearts and homes to all of them.

6 • Tracing Your Family Tree

Learn of your genealogical tree as much as is needed for the practice of active love toward blood relatives.

The Prophet Mohammed

Any significant social mobility creates renewed interest in genealogy, whether families move from country to city or simply up the social ladder. Families wonder who they are and where they came from.

There are several reasons to want to know our forebears: the personal rewards (it strengthens kinship ties), a sense of security (isn't it nice to know we belong), and a sense of pride (don't let the family down).

In the past ten years, **horizontal** (or **parallel**) **genealogy** has become the vogue. Experts study overlapping pedigrees to show that we are all members of the largest kinship group in existence—the family of man. Horizontal genealogy creates some strange bedfellows. For instance, Jimmy Carter and Richard Nixon are sixth cousins, while Richard Nixon and George Bush are tenth cousins once removed. Wouldn't that make for an interesting family reunion?

The fact that so many famous Americans are related is not surprising when you consider that 82 percent of all Americans have at least one ancestral line which is of English, Welsh, Scottish, or Irish background.

- More than 100,000 people are known to be descendants of England's Edward III, and through Edward are related to many royal lines of the Middle Ages.

- In ancient China and Japan, ancestors became personal family gods. Deceased forebears were believed to oversee and influence events on earth, and had responsibility for continuing filial piety and harmony among the living.
- Islamic countries consider the study of ancestry important because their prophet, Mohammed, taught them to "Learn of your genealogical tree as much as is needed for the practice of active love toward blood relatives."
- In certain African tribes, an ancestor's status in the hereafter depends upon the memory of the living. Every family makes a concentrated effort to think highly of the dead so that the quality of afterlife for the deceased will be enhanced. The expression "Don't speak ill of the dead" may have originated here.
- In Ireland, the Irish Genealogical Association plays host to family reunions every summer. The lure of the Emerald Isle is enough to bring hundreds of aunts, uncles, and cousins to Ireland.

Family history

Prior to the twelfth century, Western ancestral history was oral, and belonged to the realm of story-tellers and balladeers. When family history needed to be written, clergymen took over the job. Many a flawed character was transformed into a person of saintly proportions with the flick of a pen. We might say their acts were cleaned up. Too many people know about the dastardly deeds of a relative? No problem—simply saw off the limb from which he figuratively or literally hung. A lot of wayward kinfolk have been lopped off during careful pruning of the family tree.

Modern technology has made genealogical search faster, but the excitement remains. Locating ancestors entails the skill of Sherlock Holmes and the patience of Job. Just as you locate one elusive relative, reference to another pops up and the chase is on again.

One of the major difficulties in tracing relatives very far back in time is that the number of potential ancestors increases dramatically with each preceding generation. Everyone has 2 parents, 4 grandparents, 8 great-grandparents, 16 double greats, 32 triple greats, and 64 quadruple greats, with like doubling in every preceding generation. That would mean that in the year 400, you would need to locate some 18.5 quintillion ancestors . . . if it worked that way. That's more than the number of people who ever lived. How can that be? Common ancestors, that's how. If we could accurately trace our family tree as far back as the beginning of time, we would see how we are all interrelated. Somewhere along the way, cousins had to marry cousins whether they knew they were related or not.

Immediate sources

The old axiom about the apple never falling far from the tree isn't going to be of much help, because family apples can be found as close as next door, or clear around the world.

Start with yourself. Your first clue to your ancestry is your name. (If your family has maintained a documented family tree for generations, this advice may seem unnecessary, but for beginners it will prove invaluable.)

Write your family name at the top of the page. Next, list possible variations. Have any relatives changed their name? Is your name frequently mispronounced? Books on **onomastics** provide information on the origin, meaning, and evolution of names.

There are several different formats (placement of names, dates, interesting anecdotes) you may use. To discover the methods preferred by genealogists, and to choose those you are most comfortable with, a trip to the library is in order. A good guide is Val D. Greenwood's *The Researcher's Guide to American Genealogy,* published by the Genealogical Publishing Company.

Tracing your family's history always begins with you and your immediate family members. Elderly relatives are a wonderful source of information. Peruse old photographs, family Bibles, scrapbooks, or other records. In faded tintypes or dog-eared photos you will see reflected images of yourself. You may discover that a son who doesn't resemble anyone in the family looks exactly like a great-granduncle, or you can tell the daughter who wondered about her red hair that among family souvenirs is a strand of coppery-red hair that provided the same lovely glow to a great-great-grandmother.

A terrific source of family history is a relative by marriage. The interesting stories are often suppressed by *blood* kin, but in-laws never forget. Some of my father's greatest stories were those he told about my mother's side of the family. Story-telling sessions often ended with my father in the doghouse.

Many libraries offer seminars on the use of videotape to document family history.

Write letters to distant relatives (figuratively distant as well as physically). Provide a list of questions for them, and include a self-addressed stamped envelope to encourage their co-operation. When you receive your replies, don't forget a thank-you note.

More distant sources

When you have exhausted the more intimate family sources, contact fictive kin, friends, former neighbors, and religious institutions.

Vital statistics include birth, death, marriage, and naturalization records. By 1920 all states had begun registration of births and deaths. Prior to that time statistics were recorded in a rather haphazard manner, or not at all. As late as 1898 only seventeen states required compilation of vital statistics.

Visit the county Register of Deeds office to study contracts, deeds, leases, maps, and mortgages. Surrogate, Probate, or Orphans Courts are the place to examine copies of wills, adoption papers, changes of name, and petitions for guardianship.

State archives have higher court papers, census enumerations, and older vital records. Federal records contain census, land, court, immigration, and military information.

The Church of Jesus Christ of Latter-day Saints has the largest collection of genealogical information in the world. Contact the Family History Library (The Church of Jesus Christ of Latter-day Saints), Genealogical Department, Dept. P, 35 N. West Temple Street, Salt Lake City, Utah 84150-0001.

The National Archives sponsors an annual genealogical seminar. Classes are taught by experts in the fields of census records, legal records, military history, colonial handwriting, cartography, migration patterns, oral genealogy, and so forth.

There are patriotic, lineage, and ethnic societies to aid you. In addition to well-known groups like the Daughters (Sons) of the American Revolution (D.A.R. and S.A.R.), and United Daughters of the Confederacy, there are the Spanish War Veterans, Sons of Confederate Veterans, Descendants of the Signers of the Declaration of Independence, the Ladies of the Grand Army of the Republic (for female descendants of Union soldiers), and the Aztec Club of 1847 (for descendants of servicemen of the Mexican War).

Cemeteries are sources of names, dates, and relationships.

School and college records provide excellent sources of information because applications usually list family members and dates. Since the 1920s, grammar schools have taken yearly pictures of the children and usually preserve a master photograph and a roster of names.

If all of this seems a bit much, you can hire someone to do the tedious work for you. For a list of persons certified to do genealogical research, contact the Board of Certification of Genealogists, P.O. Box 19165, Washington, D.C. 20036.

Holidays and special family events bring together several generations. Why not make a record of these wonderful times? Childhood memories surface, older relatives are available to reminisce, and children can add their impressions.

There are several computer software programs available. I like the Genealogical Management System for Home Computers (Personal Ancestral File) from the Church of Jesus Christ of

Latter-day Saints, Genealogical Department, at 50 E. North Temple Street, Salt Lake City, Utah 84150. At $35.00 the package is a bargain.

Why research?

Does it seem strange to look back in order to look forward? It shouldn't. We are who we are because of who they were. Without understanding the feelings and faults, values and virtues, joys and jobs, and sorrows and successes of your ancestors, all you have left is a series of "begats."

In Alex Haley's *Roots* there are a few sentences near the end of the book which summed up for me everything there is to say about ancestors. Mr. Haley relates a conversation between his mother and his grandmother:

> *It was the talk, I knew, that always had generated my only memories of any open friction between Mama and Grandma. Grandma would get on that subject [her ancestors] sometimes . . . and Mama always before long would abruptly snap something like, "Oh, Maw, I wish you'd stop all that old-timey slavery stuff, it's entirely embarrassing!" Grandma would snap right back, "If you don't care who and where you come from, well, I does!"*

Alex Haley is eternally grateful that his grandmother cared enough to remember, and he has spent many hours and travelled thousands of miles to connect with "kinfolk."

7 ● Kinship and the Future

When I was just a little girl,
I asked my mother, "What lies ahead?
Will there be rainbows, day after day?"
Here's what my mother said:
"Que será será (Whatever will be will be)."
Popular song from the 1950s

You've been busy, all you little earthlings. Yes, you have! The Population Institute estimates that sometime in 1986 the five billionth person was born as a "sobering symbol" of world population growth. It seems you've taken the Biblical admonishment to be "fruitful and multiply" as a sacred duty.

Whoever the new person is, or whenever the child was born, at the twilight of its lifetime its concept of "kinship" may be, in many ways, vastly different from ours. Lumped in with the scientific and technological advances that can be expected will be changes within the family itself.

Sociologists are seriously concerned whether the family will even exist in its present form. Even the customs surrounding courtship, marriage, birth, kinship, and death which we currently hold dear may languish in the graveyards of the dim, distant past. Might our grandchildren be so sophisticated and unsentimental that neither custom, nor superstition, nor tradition will embellish the special events in their lives?

In most societies, great ceremony attends birth, coming of age, marriage, and death. Humans have always managed to combine the ridiculous with the sublime when it comes to these rites of passage. Some customs are necessary, some are funny, some are sad, and some are just plain silly, but in each generation we embrace our idiosyncratic beliefs with the zeal of an itinerant tent revivalist.

Families in the future

Men and women of the future have many choices in terms of the type of family life they wish to pursue. They may choose the traditional family which in the past was just about the only game in town if they were the conventional sort, or they may choose to remain single.

Should they decide not to marry, they may exercise their option to have children either with a willing partner, with the assistance of a surrogate mother, or using donated sperm.

They might choose to live in a household of related people (kinship group), or they may be non-related persons living together for financial or emotional support. Or they may decide to live alone.

Grandparents

What will happen to the grandparents of the future? Where will tomorrow's children go to be petted like a lap-dog, pampered like an Indian pasha, stuffed with food like a Dresden goose, spoiled like bananas left too long in the back of the pantry, adored as much as any deity, and loved beyond belief?

With the number of divorces and the distances which parents must travel to find work, many children are growing up never knowing what it's like to spend time with grandparents and other kin.

In my generation, grandma's house was the place where aunts, uncles, cousins, and as many shirt-tail relatives as possible crowded on special occasions; where sleeping on the floor because all the beds were full was never a hardship; where grandmother cooked your favorite food while your parents claimed with real or mock horror, "You're going to spoil that child, and it'll take a week to get her back to normal;" where grandpa showed you his collection of war medals, and filled your head full of tall tales and adventures from when he was a boy, and Gram said, "Don't tell that child those old stories, she'll have nightmares," but Gramps told them anyway; where you got to stay up late, and, if you were real quiet, could listen to the adults talk deep into the night; where you finally fell asleep to the lullaby of their soft, murmuring voices, and awoke the next morning to the aroma of breakfast wafting under your nose.

Grandparents are turning to the courts to enforce their rights to see their grandchildren in the cases of divorce or dissension within the family. People who could never relate to their own children get a second chance through their grandchildren. The removal of the strain caused by the struggle to raise a family and maintain some semblance of sanity is over, and they can relax and give unconditional love to their grandchildren.

With so many couples remaining childless, potential grandparents are having to wait extra long for grandchildren, or facing the fact that they may never be so blessed. So far, no parents have gone to the courts asking that their child be forced to have children.

Not all grandparents want to spend time with their grandchildren. Men and women are becoming grandparents "before their time" in a lot of cases, and they have jobs, hobbies, or aging parents to care for. These grandparents choose to see their grandchildren under controlled circumstances (the child is clean, quiet, and sits still) for a few minutes. And there's nothing wrong with that choice. Just remember, the future is based on the past. Time marches on, and someday that sticky, whiney, little nuisance will grow into a fine adult who will have no time for a grandparent who, by then, may have plenty of time and want to spend some of it with an adult grandchild. Unfortunately, if no relationship was forged when the child was young, usually none will exist when the child is an adult.

Kinship, who needs it?

When all is said and done, it doesn't really matter how kinship is figured. There are no clear-cut definitions which must be adhered to. Whether your society calculates degrees of cousinhood, and another refuses to accept the existence of such a relationship; whether you say great-aunt, and I say grandaunt; whether kinship is calculated bilaterally (affiliated with relatives both maternal and paternal), or unilaterally (connected mainly with either father or mother); whether descent is traced matrilineally (through the mother) or patrilineally (through the father), or even ambilineally (the individual is given a choice of which heritage to choose); whether one family traces their genealogical background for centuries and another can't locate a single grandparent . . . none of it matters beyond the fact that kinship is a basic organizing principle. Kinship is the unifying ingredient of family life in all societies.

Kinship places us in a network of status and resources, rights and responsibilities, plus giving and receiving of assistance in times of need, along with rejoicing in times of happiness and tears in times of grief. Even if any and all kinship functions can be taken over by institutions, kinship remains important.

What really matters about kinship are the emotions, the overlapping relationships, the interaction between generations (the loving as well as the feuding), and the knowledge of our heritage. These are the reasons why people research their ancestors, diagram family trees, and hold family reunions.

Kinship, who needs it? Indeed, we all do.

Epilogue

O what a tangled web we weave!

When I wrote to my cousin, Moody Smith, about my intention to write a book regarding kinship and degrees of relationship, he answered by telling me a story that could have happened in the South of not so long ago, when families were started at such an early age that it was difficult for a stranger to distinguish parent from child.

Moody told me the tale of Ferd, a widower, and his only son, Roscoe, who lived with him. Ferd dug ginseng roots, raised a little garden patch, and collected commodity cheese and dried milk. Jim-Bob, a neighbor two hills over, had a thriving business and Roscoe worked for him. Roscoe didn't report his wages because his job mostly consisted of carrying hundred-pound sacks of sugar through the woods.

The only women for several miles around belonged to Jim-Bob: his wife Roxie, and their almost-ripe daughter, Trixie. Each day at lunch time Roxie and Trixie would come down from the house and bring a platter of hot baloney sandwiches for Jim-Bob and Roscoe to eat.

Roscoe knew the business pretty well by the time the still blew up and took Jim-Bob with it. Roscoe quickly wooed and won Roxie, garnering for himself a business, a family, and hot baloney sandwiches three times a day.

Ferd started hanging around, and at night the four of them would sit around, play cards, and tell ghost stories. On the day that Trixie finished turning ripe, Ferd was right there to pick her—the two of them hopped in Jim-Bob's old pickup truck, drove over the state line and got married. Both women conceived shortly thereafter. In due time, Roxie gave birth to Bubba, and Trixie had Buster.

Roscoe was very happy. The only fly in the ointment was that Ferd seemed content to just sit back and let Roscoe support him, all the while eating Roxie's hot baloney sandwiches. Remembering the way Jim-Bob had gone, Roscoe determined to make a will—and that's when his life changed. He tried not to think about his situation, for each time he did, he began drinking his profits.

"How in the world can I provide for my daddy if I cut my shiftless son-in-law out of my will? My daddy is married to my wife's daughter, therefore he is my son-in-law. My stepdaughter, Trixie, is my stepmother. She is Roxie's daughter, but because she is my daddy's wife, she's also Roxie's mother-in-law. Trixie is Ferd's wife, but because she's my daughter, she is also Ferd's granddaughter. Little Bubba is my son, but because he is my stepmother's brother, he is also my uncle—I'm my own son's nephew.

Little Buster is my wife's grandson, so he is my grandson, too, but because he is my daddy's boy, he is also my brother. Because he is my brother, he is Bubba's uncle—so my grandson is my son's uncle. Bubba is Trixie's brother, so he is Buster's uncle. Both of them little boys are each other's uncle. That makes Trixie Bubba's sister, grandmother, and grandaunt."

Roscoe's thoughts continued, "Ferd is my daddy, and Bubba is my son, so Ferd is Bubba's granddaddy; Ferd is married to Bubba's sister, so he is Bubba's brother-in-law. Trixie is Ferd's wife, so she is Bubba's grandmother. That makes Roxie Bubba's great-grandmother, as well as his momma. If that little boy's mother is also his great-grandmother, then I have to be his great-grandfather. And because I am my son's great-grandfather, that makes me my own grandpa. Can I really be my own grandpa?"

Roscoe scratched his head, ruminated a little, and went on, "Let me look at this from another direction. Buster is my brother and Roxie is his grandmother, so I am my brother's granddaddy. Ferd is my daddy, so that makes him Buster's great-granddaddy, too. And if my daddy is also my great-granddaddy, than I just have to be my own grandpa. Yep, that is what I am, my own grandpa."

Roscoe made a quick decision to quit thinking about the mess he had going, and he dumped his problem in the lap of a local lawyer.

There may be glaring holes in Roscoe's reasoning, but it's highly possible that at some time in the jurisprudential past, some poor judge became entangled in an intestate estate squabble (one where there was no will) in which the squabblers were interrelated in a can of worms similar to Roscoe's.

After a night of fitful sleep, the judge awoke knowing what he had to do. Early that day, he hied himself to the state legislature—where, with no thought or knowledge of concomitant regressive genes, he prevailed upon his cronies to pass laws to keep close kin from getting so close that he and his colleagues might go crazy whenever it came time to sort out the closeness.

Such is the stuff of which kinship is made.

Medical Charts

Use these charts as guides. Add more space if needed, and other relevant details.

Children

Name _____   Name _____   Name _____

Born _____   Born _____   Born _____

Died _____   Died _____   Died _____

Cause of death:

_____   _____   _____

Other health problems:

_____   _____   _____

People in the family with special talents:

_____

_____

_____

Siblings

Name _____   Name _____   Name _____

Born _____   Born _____   Born _____

Died _____   Died _____   Died _____

Cause of death:

_____   _____   _____

Other health problems:

_____   _____   _____

Self and Spouse

Name _____   Name _____

Born _____   Born _____

Died _____   Died _____

Cause of death:

_____   _____

Other health problems:

_____   _____

_____   _____

Parents

Name _____   Name _____

Born _____   Born _____

Died _____   Died _____

Cause of death:

_____   _____

Other health problems:

_____   _____

_____   _____

Grandparents

Name _____   Name _____   Name _____   Name _____

Born _____   Born _____   Born _____   Born _____

Died _____   Died _____   Died _____   Died _____

Cause of death:

_____   _____   _____   _____

Other health problems:

_____   _____   _____   _____

_____   _____   _____   _____

Great-grandparents

Name _____   Name _____   Name _____   Name _____

Born _____   Born _____   Born _____   Born _____

Died _____   Died _____   Died _____   Died _____

Cause of death:

_____   _____   _____   _____

Other health problems:

_____   _____   _____   _____

_____   _____   _____   _____

Name _____   Name _____   Name _____   Name _____

Born _____   Born _____   Born _____   Born _____

Died _____   Died _____   Died _____   Died _____

Cause of death:

_____   _____   _____   _____

Other health problems:

_____   _____   _____   _____

_____   _____   _____   _____

You will be fortunate if you can list your eight great-grandparents.